PRESENTED TO:

FROM:

OCCASION:

Our purpose at Howard Publishing is to:

- Increase faith in the hearts of growing Christians
- Inspire holiness in the lives of believers
- Instill hope in the hearts of struggling people everywhere

Because He's coming again!

Questions I'd Like to Ask God © 2004 The Forest Hills Group, LLC. All Rights Reserved
Published by: Howard Publishing Co., Inc.
3117 North 7th Street, West Monroe, Louisiana 71291-2227
howardpublishing.com
Printed in Mexico

04 05 06 07 08 09 10 11 12 13   10 9 8 7 6 5 4 3 2 1

Book concept by Anderson Thomas Design, Inc.
Cover design by Matt Lehman, interior design by Matt Lehman and Joel Anderson
Cover photography by Kristi Smith, Anderson Thomas Design, Inc.
Photography on pages 9, 14, 22, 23, 47, 58, 62 by Joel Anderson, Anderson Thomas Design, Inc.

ISBN: 1-58229-354-6

Scripture quotations not otherwise marked are taken from the HOLY BIBLE, NEW INTERNATIONAL VERSION ®. Copyright © 1973, 1978, 1984 by International Bible Society. Used by permission of Zondervan. All rights reserved. Scriptures marked KJV are taken from the Holy Bible, Authorized King James Version. Scripture quotations marked NLT are taken from the Holy Bible, New Living Translation, copyright © 1996. Used by permission of Tyndale House Publishers, Inc., Wheaton, Illinois 50189

Italics in Scripture have been added by the author for emphasis.

QUESTI?NS
I'D LIKE TO ASK
GOD

MATTHEW A. PRICE & JOEL ANDERSON

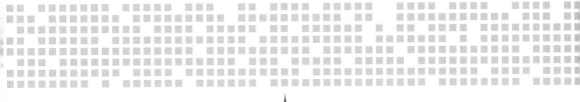

POETRY
OF THE
SOUL

WITHOUT FAITH
IT IS IMPOSSIBLE

TO PLEASE GOD,

BECAUSE ANYONE
WHO COMES TO HIM MUST
BELIEVE THAT HE EXISTS

AND THAT HE REWARDS
THOSE WHO EARNESTLY
SEEK HIM.

—HEBREWS 11:6

OK, HERE'S THE TRUTH: IT DOESN'T MATTER WHERE YOU'RE FROM

or where you're going. It doesn't matter if you're tall or short; male or female; brown, black, or white. It doesn't matter if you're headed for the Ivies, the Big Ten, the Big 12, the SEC, the ACC, trade school, or bay one at Jiffy Lube. No matter who people think you are, no matter who you think you are, no matter who you really are, the truth—the true truth—is that deep down inside of you is a desire (a longing if you want to be honest about it) to connect to something that transcends everyone you know, everything you see, and (especially) everything you are.

Well guess what? Your quest for utter certainty and spiritual absolutes can have a happy ending. But you need to know that, despite what some people say, there is only one truth—only one path you can take that leads to total peace of mind and eternal salvation.

And how can anyone possibly know this? It's because only one faith has a Redeemer. Only one religion has a loving Creator, Jesus Christ, who gave His life so that everyone who calls on His name and believes in Him will be saved for all eternity. There are no final exams, no feats of strength, no special diets, no long hours chanting and staring at the ceiling. Just ask and believe. That's it.

Of course, as with most things that are simple, there are layers of complexity in the Christian life that a

thousand lifetimes can't uncover. In fact, discovering different facets of who God is and why He created us makes Christianity a daily, moment-by-moment joy. That's why Poetry of the Soul isn't a typical guided-journaling series. Sure, it's designed to help you discover who you are in God's eyes, but more importantly, it will help you grow to know Him and love Him more deeply.

There's another important point that should be made. Poetry of the Soul doesn't treat young people like, well . . . they're young. Yes, the graphics are cool and your bookstore probably displays their copies in the youth section. But truthfully the whole idea of treating anyone between the ages of thirteen and nineteen as anything less than a fully functioning human being has only been an accepted viewpoint (and a rather condescending one at that) for the last fifty years or so.

Look in the Bible. Nowhere do you find special consideration given for a young person's age when it comes to their understanding of what is true and perfect and good. Nowhere is someone told, "Well, since you're only sixteen, you can't have clearly formed opinions on what's right and wrong, and so we won't hold you responsible for your actions."

Look at American history. In almost every era, with recent exceptions, there has been an age of accountability when a child passes into adulthood. At that point they would be expected to help on the family farm, to bear arms to protect their community, and to worship with their parents. While they probably enjoyed the company of other young people, they weren't shuffled off into youth groups at church, and they didn't think they should wait until after they'd graduated from college or got a full-time job to start acting responsibly. They were vital members of society and were expected to conduct themselves as such.

There is no better example of this than the way God called young people to do and believe great things in both the Old and New Testaments. As a young boy Samuel heard God's voice and knew that he was meant for a lifetime of ministry. God chose Mary, most likely at the age of sixteen or seventeen, to be the mother of Jesus.

If God held young people in such high regard thousands of years ago, why doesn't He feel the same today? The short answer is that He does! Any person of any age who seeks God will find Him. Anyone who desires to know why they were created and what God's purpose is for their life can find out by simply and earnestly asking, seeking, and believing.

And that's the purpose behind Poetry of the Soul. It's our desire to help young people in their search for answers that pop culture and false religions are unable to provide. It's our mission to equip young people to think for themselves, to take up positions of leadership, and to set an example of godliness for their lost and confused peers.

Most of the journal pages require deep and personal reflection. As you fill in these lines, read the accompanying text first and then answer the questions with wisdom and maturity.

And remember: If you're past the age of thirteen, then you're a young adult. It's time to think like one, to act like one, to serve like one, and to lead like one. We pray that Poetry of the Soul will help you clarify and affirm your convictions as you begin the exciting journey that awaits you.

QUESTIONS I'D LIKE TO ASK GOD

You've got questions.

Lots and lots of questions. And boy, oh boy, do people have answers. Lots and lots of answers. It should be a perfect world, right? Well, unfortunately, the answer to that question is no.

The problem is that most people base their view of the world on how they feel at that particular moment or what some celebrity says on TV or the latest mind-enhancing book from some therapist with a bad accent and an even worse haircut. Here's a tip: Any philosophy that can be summarized on an infomercial and any religion that says you can work your way to heaven (and in some cases back to earth again) can only answer the question of how much money is in your pocket.

Oh yeah, and how much money is in that jar on your shelf. Other than that, it's all just a lot of hot air and cheesy music.

The truth is that if something isn't eternally true—if it doesn't last forever and it never changes—then it's meaningless. Only Christianity has a God who always has been and always will be, who spoke the universe into existence and who came to earth as a man to live and die and rise again to atone for the sins of the world. Jesus Christ is the only answer to the ultimate question: Who can save my soul and give me the assurance of salvation?

Of course that doesn't mean you don't have a lot of other, shall we say, "peripheral" questions. The purpose of *Questions I'd Like to Ask God* is to provide a personal forum of sorts to help you begin digging into Scripture and start

opening your heart to God through prayer. The journaling pages are for you to write down your thoughts, to note key verses that are meaning-ful, and to record answered prayers.

God created us with inquisitive minds so that we would grow in knowledge, in discernment (good judgment), and in a deeper relationship with Him. That's what this book will help you to do—grow through asking questions. Jesus said,

> Ask and it will be given to you; seek and you will find; knock and the door will be opened to you. For everyone who asks receives; he who seeks finds; and to him who knocks, the door will be opened.
> —Matthew 7:7–8

In other words, *Questions I'd Like to Ask God* is really an unfinished road map to help you begin your lifelong spiritual journey. So don't be discouraged if one question leads to another; no journey worth taking is finished as soon as it starts. The one thing you can be sure of is that the One who is guiding you along the way will never leave you stuck, alone, and wondering where to turn next.

Q: Why am I here?

This age-old question (asked by everyone who has ever lived) is one of the first steps in a lifelong journey of self-discovery.

A: Why do you think God put you here?

Jesus often answered a question by asking a question in return. He did this to get to the heart of the real issue and make people examine themselves. Sometimes He did it to point them in a better direction than where their original question was headed.

When a tiny acorn falls into the tall grass, it doesn't ask, "Why did I have to fall here?" It puts out some roots and starts growing. Soon it is taller than the grass or anything else around it. God planted you exactly where He wants you. So sprout where you are and start growing toward the Light!

Q: WHO AM I?

A: You are GOD'S CREATION, designed to live in a loving relationship with Him forever.

READ ABOUT IT

"Love one another, for love comes from God. Everyone who loves has been born of God and knows God. Whoever does not love does not know God, because God is love." (1 John 4: 7–8)

PRAY ABOUT IT

"O Lord, shine Your light from heaven upon me. Bless and keep me in Your care so that I can be a witness of Your mercy and love to everyone I meet. Help me to recognize that I am a person of great worth. And show me, I pray, the purpose for which I was created. Amen."

> We are all pencils in the hand of a writing God, who is sending love letters to the world.
>
> —Mother Teresa

WRITE ABOUT IT

Why do you think God put you here?

_____

_____

_____

_____

_____

_____

_____

_____

_____

_____

_____

_____

_____

_____

_____

Ponder this: Why were you born in this time in history and not 800 years ago in some other place, such as a remote jungle?

Q: WHAT DOES IT MEAN TO BE CREATED IN THE IMAGE OF GOD?

A: YOU HAVE THE CHARACTERISTICS OF GOD.

READ ABOUT IT

"So God created people in his own image; God patterned them after himself; male and female he created them. God blessed them and told them, 'Multiply and fill the earth and subdue it. Be masters over the fish and birds and all the animals.'" (Genesis 1:27-28 NLT)

PRAY ABOUT IT

"O Lord, You gave me life. You created me in Your image. Help me to remember that I am Your child and that I have been adopted into an eternal family through the sacrificial death and glorious resurrection of Your Son, Jesus Christ. Amen."

WRITE ABOUT IT

What are some characteristics of God?

DO YOU EVER WONDER WHAT GOD LOOKS LIKE? WHAT DO THE SONGS OF ANGELS SOUND LIKE? WHAT WILL WE LOOK LIKE IN HEAVEN?

Q: WHAT DOES GOD EXPECT OF ME?

A: HE EXPECTS YOU TO WALK CLOSELY WITH HIM THROUGHOUT YOUR LIFE AND INTO ETERNITY.

READ ABOUT IT

"Work hard so God can approve you. Be a good worker, one who does not need to be ashamed and who correctly explains the word of truth." (2 Timothy 2:15 NLT)

PRAY ABOUT IT

"O Lord, help me to be a good steward of all that You have given me. Help me to show kindness and mercy to others just as You have shown patience and love toward me. I ask, too, that You will renew my faith each day so I can share the Good News of salvation with many others. Amen."

WRITE ABOUT IT

List some of your talents, resources, and abilities.
How are you using them to honor God and point others to Him?

_____

_____

_____

_____

_____

_____

_____

_____

_____

_____

_____

_____

_____

_____

_____

_____

_____

DO YOU EVER WONDER WHAT GOD THINKS ABOUT AS HE WATCHES YOU?
DOES HE EVER LAUGH? DO THE CHOICES YOU MAKE CAUSE HIM TO BE
SAD AND DISAPPOINTED OR PLEASED?

Is there life on other planets?

Will we get to visit other galaxies after we die?

What do dogs dream about?

Why did God create mosquitoes and poison ivy?

Cats have catnip, so why don't dogs have dognip?

Will I see my pets again in heaven?

How much money is enough?

As a child, could Jesus win every game He played?

Is there another word for thesaurus?

Will there be food in heaven?

God invented humor, so what does He think is funny?

Why does God allow evil to happen?

When I'm in heaven, will I be able to see loved ones who are still on earth?

Does the universe have an edge? If so, what's on the other side of it?

What did God do before He created the universe?

Q: WHY DO MY PRAYERS GO UNANSWERED?

A: God answers every prayer, but the answers may not always be what you are hoping for. Sometimes the answer is yes, no, or wait. Or sometimes He needs to change our hearts because we are asking for the wrong things.

READ ABOUT IT

"The reason you don't have what you want is that you don't ask God for it. And even when you do ask, you don't get it because your whole motive is wrong—you want only what will give you pleasure." (James 4:2–3 NLT)

PRAY ABOUT IT

"O Lord, help me to have a pure heart filled with good intentions when I pray. Don't let me fall into a rut of repeating the same words over and over, vainly hoping that I can influence when and how You will respond. You know my needs before I even say them. Let me walk in faith with the knowledge and understanding that You will answer my prayers in Your perfect timing and according to Your divine will. Amen."

WRITE ABOUT IT

What are some prayers you feel have gone "unanswered"?

_____

_____

_____

_____

_____

_____

_____

_____

_____

_____

_____

_____

_____

_____

_____

_____

DO YOU EVER WONDER IF GOD IS AMUSED WITH SOME OF THE PRAYERS
HE RECEIVES FROM HUMANS? HOW ABOUT YOUR OWN PRAYERS?

Q: HOW CAN I KNOW GOD'S WILL FOR MY LIFE?

A: Obey Him and be faithful with the little things He has already entrusted to you. If you are faithful with small things, He will entrust you with bigger things. He will unfold His will for your life one step at a time. God rarely lights up the entire path with a giant spotlight on the finish line. Rather, He usually shines enough light on the next steppingstone, so we can learn to trust Him and walk with Him each step of the way.

READ ABOUT IT

"We can make our plans, but the LORD determines our steps." (Proverbs 16:9 NLT)

PRAY ABOUT IT

"O Lord, thank You for working in me and entrusting me with so much. Please give me the strength to use what You've given me and the faith to trust Your perfect will for all my plans. I pray for an obedient and humble heart, Father, so that I can do great things for Your kingdom. Amen."

> When the eyes of the soul looking out meet the eyes of God looking in, heaven has begun right here on this earth.
>
> —A. W. Tozer

WRITE ABOUT IT

What small things (possessions, relationships, opportunities, talents, etc.) has God entrusted to you?

Ponder this: What would it have been like to be Noah? How would you have reacted if God told you to build an ark?

HOW MANY GRAINS OF SAND ARE ON THIS PLANET?

HOW MANY LIVING CREATURES CRAWL ON THE GROUND, FLY THROUGH THE AIR, AND SWIM IN THE SEAS?

How many stars are there in the universe?

HOW MANY PEOPLE HAVE LIVED AND DIED SINCE THE BEGINNING OF THE WORLD?

How can God know the thoughts of everyone at all times?

You alone are the LORD. You made the heavens, even the highest heavens, and all their starry host, the earth and all that is on it, the seas and all that is in them. You give life to everything, and the multitudes of heaven worship you.

—Nehemiah 9:6

Q: What is God like?

Your answer to this question reveals a lot more about yourself than it says about God. God is so much more than anyone can imagine. We often "put God in a box" or define Him by our own limited ideas.

A: What does the Bible say He's like?

The Bible has many names for God the Father, God the Son, and God the Spirit. Each name reveals a bit of His infinite character.

NAMES OF GOD THE FATHER

ABHIR: Mighty One
ADONAI: Master or Lord
EL-BERITH: God of the Covenant
EL-GIBHOR: Mighty God
EL-OLAM: Everlasting God
EL ELYON: Most High
EL ROI: God of Seeing
EL SHADDAI: God Almighty
ELOHIM: God
EYALUTH: Strength
GAOL: Redeemer
JEHOVAH: Yahweh, The covenant name of God
   The Self-Existent One, I AM WHO I AM
JEHOVAH ELOHIM: Lord God
JEHOVAH-JIREH: The Lord Will Provide
JEHOVAH-M'KADDESH: The Lord Who Sanctifies
JEHOVAH-NISSI: The Lord Our Banner
JEHOVAH-ROHI: The Lord Our Shepherd
JEHOVAH-ROPHE: The Lord Who Heals
JEHOVAH-SABAOTH: The Lord of Hosts
JEHOVAH-SHALOM: The Lord Our Peace
JEHOVAH-SHAMMAH: The Lord Is There
JEHOVAH-TSIDKENU: The Lord Our
   Righteousness
KADOSH: Holy One
KANNA: Jealous (zealous)
MAGEN: Shield
PALET: Deliverer
SHAPHAT: Judge
TSADDIQ: Righteous One
YESHA: (Y'shua) Savior
ZUR: God Our Rock

NAMES OF GOD THE SON

Advocate, Ancient of Days, Anointed One, Branch, The Bread of Life, Chief Apostle, Chief Cornerstone, Christ, Counselor, Daystar, Deliverer, Everlasting Father, The First and Last, Firstborn, Great High Priest, Great Physician, Guardian of Our Souls, Head of the Body, I Am, Immanuel, Jesus, Judge, King, King of Kings, Lamb of God, The Light of the World, Living Water, Lord God Almighty, Lord of Lords, Master, Mighty God, Pioneer and Perfector of Our Faith, Potentate, Prince of Peace, The Resurrection and the Life, Rock, Root of Jesse, Savior, Shepherd, Shepherd of the Sheep, Stone, The Way, Truth, and the Life, Wonderful

NAMES OF GOD THE HOLY SPIRIT

Advocate, Baptizer, Comforter, Counselor, Sanctifier, Spirit of Christ, Spirit of God, Spirit of Grace, Spirit of Holiness, Spirit of Life, Spirit of Mercy, Spirit of Truth, Strengthener

Q: WHY DOESN'T GOD MAKE HIMSELF VISIBLE, SO EVERYONE CAN SEE HIM AND BELIEVE IN HIM?

A: It seems that God loves mysteries that require us to trust Him, seek after Him, and go deeper in our pursuit of Him. After all, if we could find out all there is to know in this life, why would we yearn for heaven? If we could come to God on our own, why would we need faith? There are all kinds of questions that God has placed in our way to make us either doubt Him through our own logic or accept Him through faith. Here's an example: "What's the deal with dinosaurs? They aren't mentioned in the Garden of Eden, they weren't on the ark, and your science teacher says they were here before humans."

READ ABOUT IT

"It is written, 'I will destroy the wisdom of the wise; the intelligence of the intelligent I will frustrate.'" (1 Corinthians 1:19)

"The foolishness of God is wiser than man's wisdom, and the weakness of God is stronger than man's strength." (1 Corinthians 1:25)

"Then Jesus told him [Thomas], 'Because you have seen me, you have believed; blessed are those who have not seen and yet have believed.'" (John 20:29)

Read the whole story of Thomas in John 20:19–31.

PRAY ABOUT IT

"Lord, give me faith to believe in You, even if I can't see You. Amen."

WRITE ABOUT IT

What are some ways God "shows Himself" to you every day (nature, His Word, answered prayers)?

DO YOU EVER WONDER WHAT YOU'LL SAY TO GOD THE FIRST TIME
YOU MEET HIM IN PERSON? WHAT WILL IT BE LIKE TO HUG JESUS?

Q: DO ALL RELIGIONS EVENTUALLY LEAD TO THE SAME GOD?

A: JESUS ANSWERED, "I AM THE WAY AND THE TRUTH AND THE LIFE. NO ONE COMES TO THE FATHER EXCEPT THROUGH ME." (JOHN 14:6)

READ ABOUT IT

"We know that there is only one God, the Father, who created everything, and we exist for him. And there is only one Lord, Jesus Christ, through whom God made everything and through whom we have been given life." (1 Corinthians 8:6 NLT)

"Enter through the narrow gate. For wide is the gate and broad is the road that leads to destruction, and many enter through it. But small is the gate and narrow the road that leads to life, and only a few find it." (Matthew 7:13–14)

PRAY ABOUT IT

"O Lord, in this age of total acceptance and blind tolerance—an age that despises Your truth and criticizes anyone who claims You as their Redeemer—I pray that You will give me the courage to stand up and declare that You are the one true God. Protect me, too, Father, from the arguments of false religions and fake gods. Amen."

WRITE ABOUT IT

If someone asked you how they could get to heaven, what would you tell them?

_____

_____

_____

_____

_____

_____

_____

_____

_____

_____

_____

_____

_____

_____

_____

_____

DO YOU EVER WONDER WHAT NON-CHRISTIANS EXPERIENCE AND
COMPREHEND AT THE MOMENT AFTER THEIR LIFE HAS ENDED?

QUESTIONS TO PONDER

WISDOM FROM PROVERBS

Q: Everyone has advice. How do I know who is right?

A: Trust in the LORD with all your heart
and lean not on your own understanding;
in all your ways acknowledge him,
and he will make your paths straight.

—Proverbs 3:5-6

Q: Everyone says it's not WHAT you know,
but WHO you know that's important. Is this true?

A: The fear of the LORD is the beginning of wisdom,
and knowledge of the Holy One is understanding.

—Proverbs 9:10

Q: Everyone says love, beauty, and riches will make
a person live happily ever after. Is this true?

A: There is a way that seems right to a man,
but in the end it leads to death.

—Proverbs 14:12

BONUS: WHICH OF THESE PROVERBS ARE NOT IN THE BIBLE?
1. Cleanliness is next to godliness.
2. God helps those who help themselves.
3. Pride goes before a fall.

ANSWER: #1 & #2

WRITE ABOUT IT

Which of these proverbs best applies to you? Why?

Q: HAS ANYONE EVER SEEN GOD AND LIVED TO TELL ABOUT IT?

A: MOSES DID—WELL, SORT OF.

READ ABOUT IT

"Then Moses had one more request. 'Please let me see your glorious presence,' he said.

The LORD replied, 'I will make all my goodness pass before you, and I will call out my name, "the LORD," to you. I will show kindness to anyone I choose, and I will show mercy to anyone I choose. But you may not look directly at my face, for no one may see me and live.' The LORD continued, 'Stand here on this rock beside me. As my glorious presence passes by, I will put you in the cleft of the rock and cover you with my hand until I have passed. Then I will remove my hand, and you will see me from behind. But my face will not be seen.'" (Exodus 33:18–23 NLT)

PRAY ABOUT IT

"O Lord, I praise Your holy name—for You and You alone are worthy to be praised; for You and You alone are eternal, all-powerful, and all-knowing. Help me to seek You all of my life so that one day I may stand before You in heaven and see You face to face. Amen."

WRITE ABOUT IT

God shows us glimpses of His glory in a sunset, a baby's smile, a gentle breeze, or a bird's song. What are some ways you have caught a glimpse of God's glory?

_____

_____

_____

_____

_____

_____

_____

_____

_____

_____

_____

_____

_____

_____

DO YOU EVER WONDER HOW LONG THE LINE WILL BE IN HEAVEN TO TALK TO FAMOUS BIBLE HEROES LIKE JONAH, PETER, OR PAUL? WHAT WILL YOU SAY TO THEM?

Q: WHERE IS ORDER IN A WORLD THAT APPEARS TO BE SO RANDOM?

A: God is a God of order. Seasons change on schedule, a perfect baby is formed in nine months from two individual cells, planets orbit precisely in a solar system. God has a very intelligent plan and a powerful purpose at work in everything, no matter how random things may appear on the surface.

READ ABOUT IT

" 'Go out and stand before me on the mountain,' the LORD told him. And as Elijah stood there, the LORD passed by, and a mighty windstorm hit the mountain. It was such a terrible blast that the rocks were torn loose, but the LORD was not in the wind. After the wind there was an earthquake, but the LORD was not in the earthquake. And after the earthquake there was a fire, but the LORD was not in the fire. And after the fire there was the sound of a gentle whisper." (1 Kings 19:11–12 NLT)

PRAY ABOUT IT

"O Lord, sometimes I feel so insignificant and that nobody cares about me. Please help me to remember that You delight in every detail of my life. In a world that appears chaotic, I pray that You will direct my thoughts, words, and deeds so that my life will be in harmony with Your perfect will. I ask, O Lord, for Your reassuring whisper and Your steady guiding hand. Amen."

WRITE ABOUT IT

What are the most chaotic things in your life? Over what areas of your life do you have the least control?

_____

_____

_____

_____

_____

_____

_____

_____

_____

_____

_____

_____

_____

_____

_____

_____

_____

Do you ever wonder what it would have been like to be with God at the creation of the universe? What would it be like to watch a whole galaxy being made from nothing?

Q: DOES GOD REALLY SEND PEOPLE TO HELL?

A: YES, AND HE REALLY BRINGS PEOPLE TO HEAVEN.

READ ABOUT IT

"Don't be afraid of those who want to kill you. They can only kill your body; they cannot touch your soul. Fear only God, who can destroy both soul and body in hell." (Matthew 10:28 NLT)

"Do not let your hearts be troubled. Trust in God; trust also in me. In my Father's house are many rooms; if it were not so, I would have told you. I am going there to prepare a place for you. And if I go and prepare a place for you, I will come back and take you to be with me that you also may be where I am." (John 14:1–3)

PRAY ABOUT IT

"O Lord, You have saved me from eternal darkness through the death and resurrection of Your Son, my Savior, Jesus Christ. I can never repay You for the debt of my sins. I can only thank and praise You, both now and forever, that You paid the price for me. Amen."

WRITE ABOUT IT

Where are you going after you die? How can you be sure?

_____

_____

_____

_____

_____

_____

_____

_____

_____

_____

_____

_____

_____

_____

DO YOU EVER WONDER WHAT IT'S LIKE IN HELL? WHO WILL BE THERE? WHAT KINDS OF REGRETS AND SORROW MUST THE LOST BE FEELING?

IF YOU COULD ASK EACH OF THE FOLLOWING
ONE QUESTION, WHAT WOULD IT BE?

Adam or Eve:

An angel:

Jesus:

The Virgin Mary:

The president of the United States:

Your worst enemy:

Your best friend:

Your favorite movie star:

Your favorite musician:

Your favorite athlete:

Other:

Q: WHERE IS GOD WHEN I SEE SO MUCH EVIL AROUND THE WORLD?

A: He's right where He always is—everywhere at all times. God created mankind with a free will to choose good or evil; to love Him or reject Him. At times, God intervenes to stop evil, but at other times, He allows it to go on for reasons that only He knows. In the end, God will prevail, and everyone who ever lived will face judgment for his or her deeds.

READ ABOUT IT

"Don't worry about the wicked. Don't envy those who do wrong. For like grass, they soon fade away. Like springtime flowers, they soon wither. Trust in the LORD and do good. Then you will live safely in the land and prosper. Take delight in the LORD, and he will give you your heart's desires." (Psalm 37:1–4 NLT)

PRAY ABOUT IT

"O Lord, I know that the evil I see in the world will one day pass away. I know that You are ultimately in control. Help me remember that even though I may have many trials and sorrows now or in the future, You have overcome the world for me. Amen."

WRITE ABOUT IT

Describe something evil you have seen or heard about lately. How do you think God feels about it?

_____

_____

_____

_____

_____

_____

_____

_____

_____

_____

_____

_____

_____

_____

_____

_____

_____

_____

DO YOU EVER WONDER WHAT IT WILL BE LIKE FOR PEOPLE WHO HAVE LIVED EVIL LIVES TO MEET GOD FACE TO FACE AND EXPLAIN THEIR ACTIONS?

Q: WHERE IS GOD WHEN INNOCENT PEOPLE SUFFER?

A: First of all, nobody is innocent. ("All have sinned and fall short of the glory of God." [Romans 3:23]) But even when good people suffer, it doesn't mean they are being punished. There is a difference between discipline and punishment. Discipline guides and refines a person. Punishment makes someone pay for a wrong they have committed. So where is God when His people suffer? He is near them, ready to comfort, heal, and guide them through their trials so they can become more fit for heaven.

READ ABOUT IT

"Blessed are the poor in spirit: for theirs is the kingdom of heaven. Blessed are they that mourn: for they shall be comforted. Blessed are the meek: for they shall inherit the earth. Blessed are they which do hunger and thirst after righteousness: for they shall be filled. Blessed are the merciful: for they shall obtain mercy. Blessed are the pure in heart: for they shall see God. Blessed are the peacemakers: for they shall be called the children of God. Blessed are they which are persecuted for righteousness' sake: for theirs is the kingdom of heaven. Blessed are ye, when men shall revile you, and persecute you, and shall say all manner of evil against you falsely, for my sake. Rejoice, and be exceeding glad: for great is your reward in heaven: for so persecuted they the prophets which were before you." (Matthew 5:3–12 KJV)

PRAY ABOUT IT

"O Lord, You have promised to care for the sick and the poor, for the elderly and the despised, for those who grieve and for those who are persecuted for Your sake. I truly believe that You do not turn Your back on the less fortunate and that You listen to their cries for help. As for me, Father, I pray that I can be a source of comfort to those in need. I pray that I can give 'a cup of cold water' in Your name so that others can see Your compassion through my actions. Amen."

WRITE ABOUT IT

Do you know of anyone who is suffering? Write down a prayer for them.

_____

_____

_____

_____

_____

_____

_____

_____

_____

_____

_____

_____

_____

_____

_____

_____

_____

Do you ever wonder what it must feel like for God to watch evil people prosper while good people suffer?

Q: WHEN WILL JESUS COME BACK?

A: When someone asked Him about the last days, Jesus said in Matthew 24:36–37, "No one knows about that day or hour, not even the angels in heaven, nor the Son, but only the Father. As it was in the days of Noah, so it will be at the coming of the Son of Man."

READ ABOUT IT

"And then at last, the sign of the coming of the Son of Man will appear in the heavens, and there will be deep mourning among all the nations of the earth. And they will see the Son of Man arrive on the clouds of heaven with power and great glory. And he will send forth his angels with the sound of a mighty trumpet blast, and they will gather together his chosen ones from the farthest ends of the earth and heaven." (Matthew 24:30–31 NLT)

"When the Son of Man returns, it will be like it was in Noah's day. In those days before the Flood, the people were enjoying banquets and parties and weddings right up to the time Noah entered his boat. People didn't realize what was going to happen until the Flood came and swept them all away. That is the way it will be when the Son of Man comes." (Matthew 24:37–39 NLT)

PRAY ABOUT IT

"O Lord, whether You return today or many years from now, I pray that You will guide and direct me each and every day so that I will use my time wisely for Your glory. I pray also, Father, that my words and actions will be a reflection of Your presence in my life so that others will come to know You as their Lord and Savior. Amen."

WRITE ABOUT IT

Do you feel like you are ready for Jesus to return? Why or why not?

_____
_____
_____
_____
_____
_____
_____
_____
_____
_____
_____
_____
_____
_____
_____
_____
_____

DO YOU EVER WONDER WHAT IT WILL BE LIKE WHEN JESUS RETURNS AND TAKES
ALL BELIEVERS TO HEAVEN? WHAT WILL OTHERS THINK WHO ARE LEFT BEHIND?

Q: Where am I going?

There were two boys standing at the edge of a snowy field. They wanted to see who could make the straightest set of footprints across the field. One boy looked at his feet, carefully lining up each step in front of the next until he reached the other side. The other boy fixed his eyes on a fence post on the other side of the field and headed straight for it.

A: Where are you headed?

The first boy's tracks swerved this way and that. He actually veered diagonally, taking twice as long to reach the other side as his pal did. The second boy's tracks were almost perfectly straight.

Keep your eyes set on your goal, and you will get there a lot quicker. But even more important, be sure that the goal you set out to reach is a worthy one.

"He holds victory in store for the upright, he is a shield to those whose walk is blameless, for he guards the course of the just and protects the way of his faithful ones." (Proverbs 2:7–8)

Q: HOW DO I LEARN TO FORGIVE OTHERS WHEN THEY HAVE HURT ME?

A: Practice, practice, practice. When one of Jesus' disciples asked Him, "Lord, how many times shall I forgive my brother when he sins against me? Up to seven times?" Jesus answered, "I tell you, not seven times, but seventy-seven times." (Matthew 18:22)

READ ABOUT IT

"You must make allowance for each other's faults and forgive the person who offends you. Remember, the Lord forgave you, so you must forgive others." (Colossians 3:13 NLT)

PRAY ABOUT IT

"O Lord, it's so difficult to forgive when someone has been aggressively mean and cruel. But I know that You forgave those who crucified You. This was the greatest injustice of all time, and yet You showed compassion in the midst of Your unbearable suffering. Help me to follow Your example so I can be a true witness of Your love. Amen."

IF YOUR ENEMY IS HUNGRY, GIVE HIM FOOD TO EAT; IF HE IS THIRSTY, GIVE HIM WATER TO DRINK. IN DOING THIS, YOU WILL HEAP BURNING COALS ON HIS HEAD, AND THE LORD WILL REWARD YOU.

—PROVERBS 25:21–22

WRITE ABOUT IT

Is there anyone you need to forgive? Who is it, and what have they done?

DO YOU EVER WONDER WHAT IT MUST HAVE BEEN LIKE FOR JESUS TO FORGIVE THE PEOPLE WHO CRUCIFIED HIM? HOW FORGIVING ARE YOU?

Q: HOW CAN I KEEP FROM THINKING BADLY OF PEOPLE I DON'T LIKE?

A: Do what Jesus did. Have compassion on them. Look past their bad attitudes or yucky behavior to see their pain. Most people have hidden hurts, anger, or shame that they cover up to protect themselves. Someone who is grouchy may have had their feelings hurt. Someone who is pushy or rude may have been treated as if they were unimportant. Someone who shows off may be starving for approval or affirmation. Look past the symptom to the disease and offer up healing prayers for them. Then, as God may direct you, look for ways to act like Jesus toward them.

READ ABOUT IT

"Knowing God leads to self-control. Self-control leads to patient endurance, and patient endurance leads to godliness. Godliness leads to love for other Christians, and finally you will grow to have genuine love for everyone." (2 Peter 1:6–7 NLT)

PRAY ABOUT IT

"O Lord, give me self-control over my emotions. Help me to be patient with others. Fix in me a loving heart that isn't judgmental or suspicious or critical. I thank You for Your unfailing presence in my life, and I pray that each day my relationship with You will grow stronger and deeper. Amen."

WRITE ABOUT IT

Who are some people you don't like? Why don't you like them? How can you pray for them?

DO YOU EVER WONDER WHAT OTHER PEOPLE THINK OR SAY ABOUT YOU
WHEN YOU ARE NOT AROUND? DO YOU PRAY FOR PEOPLE YOU DON'T LIKE?

Q: HOW CAN I DEVELOP A RELATIONSHIP WITH JESUS?

A: If you confess with your mouth that Jesus is Lord and believe in your heart that God raised him from the dead, you will be saved. For it is by believing in your heart that you are made right with God, and it is by confessing with your mouth that you are saved. As the Scriptures tell us, "Anyone who believes in him will not be disappointed." (Romans 10:9–11 NLT)

READ ABOUT IT

Stay in the Word.
"All Scripture is God-breathed and is useful for teaching, rebuking, correcting and training in righteousness." (2 Timothy 3:16)

Become involved in a good church home.
"Let us not give up meeting together . . . , but let us encourage one another." (Hebrews 10:25)

Be baptized.
"Go make disciples of all nations, baptizing them in the name of the Father and of the Son and of the Holy Spirit, and teaching them to obey everything I have commanded you." (Matthew 28:19–20)

PRAY ABOUT IT

"O Lord, thank You for securing my salvation. Thank You, Father, for taking the burden of my sins upon Yourself so I can spend eternity in Your presence. Thank You, my Rock and my Redeemer, that Your blood washed away my sins and that my name appears in Your Book of Life. I thank You and I praise you, both now and forever. Amen."

WRITE ABOUT IT

Describe the time you were saved. (If you have never been saved, why not confess and believe right now? What is holding you back?)

DO YOU EVER WONDER WHAT IT WOULD BE LIKE TO LIVE FOREVER, PERMANENTLY ISOLATED AND SEPARATED FROM GOD?

Q: IS IT WRONG FOR ME TO WANT FINANCIAL SECURITY?

A: Actually there is no such thing as financial security. The reality is that anything in this world can be lost, stolen, or ruined. If you are looking at money, regardless of the amount, to make you secure, you are putting your trust in a sandcastle. Look at the mightiest empires of human history—the Egyptians, the Greeks, the Romans—all of these wealthy empires have long since crumbled. Think of the richest people you know. On their deathbeds, nothing they own will buy them another day of life. And they won't be taking anything with them, either. Your best bet for security is trusting in God.

READ ABOUT IT $$$$$$$$$$$$$$$$$$$

"A person is a fool to store up earthly wealth but not have a rich relationship with God." (Luke 12:21 NLT)

"Don't store up treasures here on earth, where they can be eaten by moths and get rusty, and where thieves break in and steal. Store your treasures in heaven, where they will never become moth-eaten or rusty and where they will be safe from thieves. Wherever your treasure is, there your heart and thoughts will also be." (Matthew 6:19–21 NLT)

PRAY ABOUT IT

"O Lord, sometimes when I see people who have a lot of money, it makes me want to have what they have. Please help me to place importance on things that really matter, on things that You value. Thank You for the earthly riches You have given me. Please give me the wisdom to be a good steward and to use what I have to share Your love with others. Amen."

WRITE ABOUT IT

List some things that make you feel secure (locks, parents, savings account, etc.). How can these things fail you? How can God give you true security?

_____

_____

_____

_____

_____

_____

_____

_____

_____

_____

_____

_____

_____

Do you ever wonder what it would be like to be the richest person in the world? What would you do and buy if you had billions of dollars?

THINGS YOU **SHOULD** QUESTION

- Your motives—Why do you do and say certain things? Are you motivated by the fruit of the Spirit (love, joy, peace, patience, kindness, goodness, faithfulness, gentleness, and self control), or are you self-seeking and self-serving in what you do and say? Question why you do what you do.

- Your feelings—What if you only did something when you felt like it? You wouldn't get up and go to school on Monday morning, you wouldn't forgive others, you wouldn't ever face tough challenges and grow up. Great and noble people live beyond their feelings to act bravely when they feel scared, to forgive when they feel hurt, to have self-control when they are tempted, and to love when they won't be loved in return.

- Your beliefs—Why do you believe what you believe? Have you searched out and cross-examined your beliefs about God, heaven, and hell by studying the Bible? Some people can even misuse the Bible, taking verses out of context and twisting their meaning to suit their own beliefs. Study God's Word and ask the Holy Spirit to help you discern what is true.

- The media—What messages do movies, TV shows, songs, and advertisements tell you? They suggest that you should not be satisfied with the stuff you have—that you should want newer, cooler stuff. They tell you you aren't perfect like all of the airbrushed models; that you should be wearing the latest styles to be cool. They tell you that sex, money, and following your dreams are what will make you happy. Most of what you see and hear has been created by people who don't know God and don't believe in heaven and hell.

THINGS YOU **SHOULD NOT** QUESTION

- God's love—You are valuable and very special to God. He made you and loves you just the way you are. But He also loves you enough not to allow you to stay that way! He wants you to grow up. Often, He will use some pain or discomfort to help you grow, like a coach who makes an athlete work very hard to be fit for a race or a surgeon who must cut in order to heal. But whatever God must do to grow you, He does it because He loves you. He proved it by sending Jesus to die for your sins!

- God's Word—God gave us the Bible to teach us, guide us, and reveal Himself to us. Jesus said, "Heaven and earth will pass away, but my words will never pass away" (Matthew 24:35). The Bible is God's love letter to the world. It is a road map to heaven, and it is the final authority on all things.

Q: WHY DO I FEEL SPIRITUALLY EMPTY SOME DAYS?

A: There is an old expression that says "If you feel far away from God, guess who has moved." God will not leave you, although often we stray away from His side. Sometimes, we just get swallowed up by the worries and cares of this world and forget that He is always with us. But don't worry, we have this promise: "Be strong and courageous . . . for the LORD your God goes with you; he will never leave you nor forsake you." (Deuteronomy 31:6–7)

READ ABOUT IT

"As the deer pants for streams of water, so I long for you, O God. I thirst for God, the living God. When can I come and stand before him?" (Psalm 42:1–2 NLT)

PRAY ABOUT IT

"O Lord, I want to be filled with Your Holy Spirit. I pray that You will help me find time each day to read and meditate upon Your Word. I recognize that I will only grow as a Christian if I turn to You regularly in prayer and if I earnestly ask for Your presence in my life. Amen."

WRITE ABOUT IT

Describe a time when you felt very close to God and spiritually full.

_____

_____

_____

_____

_____

_____

_____

_____

_____

_____

_____

_____

_____

_____

_____

_____

Do you ever wonder what it must have been like to hear God's voice as clearly as Abraham, Moses, or Elijah did?

Q: IS IT WRONG TO TELL A LIE WHEN IT WON'T HURT ANYONE?

A: Who says it won't hurt anyone? One person it will hurt is you. When you lie to get what you want (approval, acceptance, or admiration, for example), you are saying that God's ways aren't good enough and won't satisfy you. If you want something so badly that you're willing to lie to get it, maybe it isn't even worth having! When you tell a lie, you violate trust, which is the basis for any good relationship. Lying will eventually make you a lonely person with no true friends.

READ ABOUT IT

"A lying tongue hates its victims, and flattery causes ruin."
(Proverbs 26:28 NLT)

PRAY ABOUT IT

"O Lord, sometimes it seems so much easier to tell a lie than to tell the truth. And sometimes I feel like I shouldn't tell the truth because it might give someone the wrong impression or hurt their feelings. Help me to control my tongue, Father. Help me to be silent when I shouldn't speak and to be honest and straightforward when I open my mouth. May the words I say be pleasing to You. Amen."

WRITE ABOUT IT

Have you ever told a "little white lie"? Have you told any big colorful lies? If you could "rewind" and have it to do over again, how would you tell the truth in these same circumstances?

PONDER THIS: WHAT WOULD IT BE LIKE IF IT WERE IMPOSSIBLE FOR ANYONE TO TELL A LIE? HOW DIFFERENT WOULD THIS WORLD BE?

Q: Are we done yet?

If you've gotten this far, you've already asked and answered a lot of questions (unless you're just peeking to see how this book ends!). Your writing hand may be cramped, and you may be mentally exhausted; but if you learned anything new about yourself, it was all worth it!

A: Have we really even started?

Like a caterpillar who has just made a nice, safe cocoon, your journey has only served to prepare you for what's next. Keep asking questions and seeking the Truth—and don't hesitate to stop and ask for directions along the way!

WRITE YOUR "FUTURE SELF" A LETTER

Keep it in a safe place so you can pull it out and read it a year from now. Give yourself a little advice about how to grow wiser. Warn yourself about some things to avoid and ask yourself some questions that can only be answered by you in the passing of time. (For example: Who will become a closer friend over the next year? How will I grow in my faith during the next year? What will be the biggest mistake I'll make?) Don't forget to put the date on it!

YOU DESIRE HONESTY
FROM THE HEART,
SO YOU CAN TEACH ME TO
BE WISE IN MY INMOST BEING.
PURIFY ME FROM MY SINS,
AND I WILL BE CLEAN;
WASH ME, AND I WILL BE
WHITER THAN SNOW.

—PSALM 51:6–7 NLT

About the Authors

Matthew A. Price, coauthor of Poetry of the Soul, is a writer, publisher, and marketing consultant. He is the author or coauthor of nearly thirty books, including The Story of Christianity, a best-selling reference work that has been translated into five languages and has sold more than 250,000 copies. Matthew's background with youth-oriented projects includes the development of The EDGE, a teen devotional Bible, The Jubilee Family Illustrated Bible, and the series Squeaky Sneaker Books. He has also contributed articles for On Track and Movin' On. Matthew and his wife, Jeanie, live in Brentwood, Tennessee, with their five children.

Joel Anderson, coauthor of Poetry of the Soul, is a designer, painter, photographer, and author. He is co-owner of Anderson Thomas Design, Inc., in Nashville, a nationally recognized graphic design firm. He has garnered an Emmy Award for his design work on a CBS children's show, a Dove Award for Best Album Cover of the Year, and several other awards for product design aimed at young people. Joel has designed and created numerous books, magazines, and pop-culture products for the music, publishing, and entertainment industries. He has authored or coauthored eleven books, which he also designed and illustrated. Joel enjoys painting, gardening, and family fun with his wife and four children.

More poetry for your soul . . .

POETRY
OF THE
SOUL

A JOURNAL FOR
ANSWERING THE QUESTION:

WHO AM I?

MATTHEW A. PRICE & JOEL ANDERSON

A BOOK TO HELP YOU
DISCOVER WHO YOU ARE

HOWARD
PUBLISHING CO.